The Fruit of the Spirit Anthology:

Taking Life's Bitter Moments and Making Them Sweet

Mary Hale
Oeinna Jackson
Valorie Tatum
Toneal M. Jackson

www.WeAreAPS.com

Table of Contents

About the Authors

Author's Note

Many times, when people hear the phrase, "The Fruit of Spirit", they associate it with something that was taught in the Bible days. The thought is that these principles no longer matter or are outdated; however, nothing could be further from the truth.

The purpose of this book is to prove that not only are these concepts still applicable, but they are highly relevant in our everyday lives. Each woman has taken the time to demonstrate how their respective fruit has played a role throughout the course of their lives. Hopefully, once you finish reading, you will understand the never-ending value they possess in your lives too!

The Scars of Yesterday: Love

A feeling of strong or constant affection for and dedication to another

When life has not raised you, it drags you, meaning if you ignore the signs of yesterday, the scars from the past will come back to haunt you. We cannot govern our destiny if we fall prey to our past. We learn from our parents, society, surroundings and each other. This is called the imitation of life.

Born into a world of sin, we are but filthy rags, we are an imitation of life. Because we ate what our parents fed us from the womb, whatever life or sin they committed while we were in the womb, we will most likely reproduce in our lifetime. We digest it emotionally, physically and spiritually; it is our inheritance. However, we don't have to stay there. There was a point in her life when she felt the love and attention from her family and her community. As a child, she thought life was good; she was always told that a child should stay in a child's place and that is how it was. But as she got older, she began to pay attention to her surroundings and sometimes life was not so good.

In her lifetime, she had seen women being beaten by their mates, people being shot down by violence, relatives dying from sickness and disease. As a child, she had to leave an environment that she felt safe in. Because of adult decisions and mistakes that were made, she never really lived as a normal child. She lived as an adult in a child's mind, so there was no band-aid for the wounds when she failed to understand the cause and effects of life. She was still bleeding because the scars of the past were still there. Her battles in life taught her how to survive; she knew how to manipulate others to get her way and to get things done.

This story is about was a woman who could hold her own. No matter what life threw at her, she considered herself a survivor. She experienced a lot of traumatic events in her past. She thought at this time in her life she should be happy; things could not be better. However, on this particular day, there was a sad, gloomy feeling. She thought to herself, what is it now?

Every person has a sequestered story, and sometimes we hold that story of unresolved issues for so long never dealing with the root of the problem. When we are in a relationship, whether with our parents, friends, mates, siblings, family members, etc. we put into each relationship what is in our heart. These are the issues of life. We also know that relationships are killed by lies, secrets, jealousy, envy, lack of consideration and deceit.

The day was gloomy and rainy as she set gazing out of her window visualizing the events that had taken place in her past. She began to think something was truly missing in her life. She felt incomplete. What is my problem? Trying to reason with herself on how she got to this point of feeling this sudden unhappiness.

Words could not explain how she felt at this moment. How and why was she so angry and bitter with herself? Why am I feeling this way? She has had this feeling in the past growing up as a child but was able to overcome it, so why is it a problem now? At that moment, it hit her. She had stopped drinking and was no longer going to the club; there seemed to be a void. She then began to realize that over the years she had been self-medicating. She overcame her issues with possessions, food, parties, alcohol, drugs, sex. She used these things to replace all of her emotions especially when it came to giving or receiving love, because of her past hurt; she never allowed anyone to get close to her.

None of the fillers she used in the past added any value to her life, neither did they reflect her or her future. She realized that she had outgrown these things and become wiser in her decision, however there was a void.

Her acceptance level for thoughtlessness and drama was unendurable. She did not need things of this nature in her life, they were not good for her psychologically or physically. There was an unhappiness, sadness in her heart. What was the void? Something was missing.

It seemed as if every emotion that could have been felt hit her all at once – anxiety, depression, heartache, grief. Somewhere in life she had lost herself. She began to question her character, her integrity, her life. This feeling took her back to her childhood. She has had the same feeling in the past when she was younger. She began to reminisce of the times when she felt alone, misused, abandoned. However, it had never affected her like it had now. She began to remember some of the events of sorrow and disappointment she experienced growing up as a child and part of her adult life. It was then that the light came on – she forgot how to love.

There was no love in her; the imitation of life had drained her. The love she remembered at a certain point in childhood had died. Her heart had turned to stone. How did she get to this place in her life?

She began to recall the things she had gone through,

things she had experienced and done in the past – things she was not so proud of, but such was life. She thought about things that were said and done to her in the past. Things she knew had nothing to do with love. In her past, she never stopped to question why things were the way they were; she was content with life. She relied on what her ancestors taught her to do and everything seemed fine.

She thought, *when we are young and experiencing life, we don't stop to question our feelings; we go with the flow of life. We experience jealousy, envy, betrayal but never think about what it does to our future. We simply go on with life – that is, until those bricks of the past that have been thrown leave us with the scars of the future.* She felt alone and resentful. These things had caused her to isolate herself. She gave a lot of thought to the moments of bitterness, anger, denial, frustration, sorrow and regret that had dominated her life in the past.

Somehow, the scars of yesterday made her feel as if she had abandoned herself. The battles she used to face left her drained. He remained silent. What would she do now? Not only had she lost the love and respect for herself, she had no idea of how the disappointment and bitterness had affected her life or what things led her to this point. Had anyone ever explained to her what it meant to love? Had she bothered to ask? Did she really understand what it is to love?

In her lifetime she had dealt with a lot of ups and downs, a lot of mistakes, turnarounds and a lot of fragmented pieces of life that weighed on her heart. Her dignity, the humility she had been through, loss of family, miscarriages, abandonment, rejection, embarrassment. She had survived through some difficult times – rocky relationships with family and friends; the mark of the choices she had made in life was now bringing back memories of the past. She went through a lifetime of having her own idea of what love was she thought she was a loving person, she thought she had learned how to love from being around family, friends and the other people she endured.

It was now that she had questions because of the situation and circumstances that she was facing at this very moment, those feelings had come back to haunt her. She somehow felt alone and abandoned, the heartache. The issue of life of the reflection she was facing in the window. With tears streaming down her face she began to question her whole life. Had she gone through life with no understanding or idea of what it really is to love someone?

After all, she had always been the stronger one, the one that was in control of all her emotions, so she thought. The one that hid her feelings from everyone else. She kept a lot of feelings to herself, her own personal feelings. She never needed a reason before to share with anyone. Why would she feel the need to discuss or share? After all, she could handle whatever came her way.

Love

There had been times in her life when she felt disgraced when her dignity and her honor had been challenged. She dealt with humiliation in her life, which led to bitterness – these things led her to isolate herself and made her feel worthless as a woman.

She questioned herself not sure if she had the capability of ever loving anyone. She had built a heart of stone, a wall that only God could tear down. Had she really loved or was she acting, pretending, mimicking, and surviving? Or was she just going with the flow of life? Was it a role she played to hide what was really going on in her life?

If someone had asked her what love was in her younger days, she probably would have said it was a happy feeling to have someone to be by her side or in her life; the need to be close to someone, to be intimate and never leave. However, life changed her outlook on the way love was supposed to be when things went the opposite direction of what she thought life would be. She was so busy with the things of life – husband, children, family members, work, etc. She forgot about love for herself. She did not have time for affection; there was work and there was survival.

She set by the window thinking about all the fragmented pieces of her life. She saw the reflection of herself. Why am I feeling this way? I am a wife, mother, daughter, sister, friend and aunt. I have always comforted and encouraged everyone else, but who was here to comfort me? She was alone looking at the reflection.

She began to question herself because she realized she had replaced love with material possessions. What is love? she wondered. Have I been looking for love in all the wrong places? What is the right or wrong way when it comes to matters of the heart? Was it really ever a time when love existed or was it really more about control and survival? She began to remember her true identity and had a life changing moment.

She said to herself, I have endured the brokenness and the hardship, and through it all somewhere in the midst of it all, I have lost myself. Because I received pain and abuse, I lived pain and abuse because it was what I was used to, it was what I knew. She never asked anybody for anything in return; she always gave of herself, never allowing anyone to comfort her, because of her past experiences.

Love can be a hurting thing when it is geared in the wrong direction. Jeremiah 17:9 says, "The heart is deceitful above all things, and desperately wicked: who can know it?" We become fearful and afraid of losing people or possessions.

There are so many types of love: love for parents, love of our mates, love of children, self-love, godly love, love for family members, siblings and friends. then there is physical love, emotional love and unconditional love.

To me, love is having a great interest and pleasure in someone, it is an intense feeling of deep affection, a strong feeling of affection and sexual attraction.

Love is when our mind extends to join with someone that is desirable to us. It's when we are secure enough to set aside self-concern and include someone else in our life AND attend to their needs. There is no such thing as 20% or 72% love, as it is not rationed out; either we love, or we don't. Love is not verbally, emotionally or mentally abusive. We do not attack someone's sense of self-worth, use insults, call names, criticize or humiliate them. We are created to love, but circumstances, caused by pain creates an environment that wears away at our hearts.

We close ourselves down and do not allow or expect anything in return. We give up everything including the love for ourselves. As some of us get older and wiser, we begin to get a reality check living a life of regret. We get angry with ourselves for allowing others to have had so much control and power over our hearts. Most of us have heard the quote "the opposite of love is fear", meaning that when we approach life, we can approach it two ways: from a place of fear or a place of love. If love is based on fear, it becomes "iffy": if I have this, if you do this, if you give me this.

Fear is an insecure self, filled with self-concern, brings up past experiences that in some ways hurt us or maybe it was unpleasant or seen as dangerous. Fear's enemy is love. Fear and love cannot abide with one another. When we act out of love, we are coming from a place of openness and peace. We are more grounded and honest.

If we are approaching life in love, we are more transparent and are likely to be more compassionate, forgiving and affectionate. When we operate out of fear, it will more than likely bring on grief, bitterness, anger and disappointment. It affects us physically, emotionally, and spiritually because bitterness is very penetrating. It bites and devours like a snake and scars everything and anything it encounters.

She thought, *Today is a new day, something has to change. I cannot go through life like this, something must change. I am no longer in agreement with my past. I am going to walk away from my mistakes and my fears.*

I Still Have Joy:
Joy
*A feeling of great pleasure
and happiness*

American gospel music singer, Tye Tribett has a song that says, "After all that I've been through, I still have my joy". Although I knew the lyrics, it took a while to understand how such a statement could be true. I'd experienced so much heartache and grief I couldn't quite make sense of those words.

A few months after I turned 21, my mother confided on me that she believed she had cancer; however, she didn't want to go through chemotherapy or radiation. She said she told me because she felt I was the only one who would understand; she didn't think my dad or sister would be able to handle the news. To me, this announcement seemed to come out of the blue, but two months later, it was confirmed that she was right. Not only did she have this dreadful disease, but it was Stage Four. So, at only 45 years old, my mother was literally in a fight for her life.

Leading up to what would be the final weeks of her life, my mother moved in with me so I could care for her. I witnessed someone who I'd always known as being super independent become relatively helpless at no fault of her own. Someone who'd always been the strength for her family now had to depend on the strength of others. She went from walking by herself to needing the assistance of a cane, then a walker, and ultimately a wheelchair. I was totally devastated watching this transition happen right before my eyes. In the midst of this though, my mother still proved to be my protector.

You see, at this time in my life, I was still estranged from my biological father. However, he'd gotten the news of my mother's terminal illness and wanted the chance to see her. This was extremely stressful for me because I'd only seen him once, and that had been four years earlier when I was 18. So now, someone I'd wanted so desperately to be in my life, wanted to come to my house, but only because my mother was dying, and she happened to live with me.

In either case, I allowed the visitation because I didn't feel I had the right to intervene. Though I was angry, this was not the time nor my place to interfere; this was about my mother. He ended up coming to my house and when he did, this 80 lb. woman who lacked the ability to walk, stumbled out of the room to stand up for me. She looked him boldly in the eyes and said, "You're not here for me. You get things right with your daughter". And with that, she stumbled her way back to her room.

We looked at each other and mutually agreed to talk. The conversation went on for about three hours. I told him why I hated him; confessed how his absence created this overwhelming sense of rejection; and finally asked why he didn't want me. I always blamed myself and felt totally repulsive because of it. I mean, how worthless was I if my own father wanted nothing to do with me?

He explained how it had nothing to do with me. That once my mother married my dad, he felt it best to let me move on with someone who would have a more consistent presence in my life. He said he'd kept up with me and my accomplishments through my grandmother. Although it made logical sense, somehow, his explanation made me feel even worse. He vowed that this time would be different, and if I would forgive him and give him another chance that he'd make good on his word. I did and so did he.

A couple of weeks later, my mother died. He was at her funeral. He called me almost every day. When he didn't call, he was at my house. We were bonding. He was there a few months later when my daughter was born. He held her and visited me to spend time with us both. I was really beginning to enjoy our relationship. But then, the unthinkable happened; just a few months after my daughter was born, he had a massive stroke and died.

Here I was still trying to adjust to my mother's death, and just ten months later, he dies. I thought that that grief was unbearable until just five months later (the day before Thanksgiving), my grandmother died. For a long time, I thought I was having a bad dream, just unable to wake up. To say I was heartbroken would be putting it mildly; lost would be more like it. I was devastated and depressed. I felt like I couldn't go on. There were times when I didn't just feel suicidal, I attempted to take my life. I felt God had betrayed me. I didn't understand the point of praying or fasting or adhering any of the biblical principles to which I'd devoted my life. It never seemed to end. Every year for 10 years straight, I lost a loved one. Not a friend, not a neighbor or co-worker, but a close family member. From 2002-2012, I lost my mother; biological father; two grandmothers; aunts; uncles; cousins; even my 18-month-old nephew.

In between deaths, I gave birth to four beautiful daughters. Many people suggested I focus on the happy moments. However, I could never seem to hold on to those moments; they seemed to quickly fade away. Much of the time, I felt myself simply existing, going through the motions of doing what I'd programmed myself to be the right thing. On the outside I was smiling, but on the inside, I was crumbling. People felt I was being ungrateful because to the public I had all these things. I was married with children; had a house; cars; and material goods. So, I should be happy, right? It was during this time of my life that I realized the difference between happiness and joy.

Happiness is typically situational, or temporary. It's based on the things you have, positive circumstances – a promotion on your job; getting a new car; being in a good place in your relationship. If something goes wrong with any of these things, then your demeanor fluctuates. Joy, on the other hand, is more innate. It's when you have a true understanding of who you are. It's embracing the greater concept of your life's purpose. It's the realization that something will always go wrong because that's the nature of life. But just as there will always be negativity, positivity will always exist too. It's your job to make a conscious effort to identify the latter.

Negativity always makes it presence felt – no announcement necessary. You can become so overwhelmed with all the bad news and negative aspects that it distracts you from the good things. I had to grow and mature to understand this lesson. I had to learn that despite the trials and tragedies, my life still had purpose. And that every day I allowed myself to be depressed and distracted (yes, it's a choice) was a day that I wouldn't accomplish what I was created to do. I learned that the devil desires to take over your mind because if he does, if he is successful in getting you to give up, then you're no longer a threat.

Understand that I am not saying you won't face obstacles or hardships. I'm not saying you won't endure pain or that you won't suffer. What I am saying is that how you handle what's presented is up to you. You can either look at it with natural eyes and allow yourself to go on an endless emotional rollercoaster filled with ups and downs (really bad when you're going through and really good in the "happy" times). Or, you can decide that no matter what happens, you will possess an attitude of gratitude. That although something unfavorable occurs, you will possess a Philippians 4:8 mindset. The mentality that encourages you to think solely on the things that are good, true, lovely and just. If you decide to embrace that mindset, you will be able to experience the best part of yourself. Then, like Tye Tribett, you too will be able to say (and mean), "After all I've been through, I still have my joy"!

Joy

Coaching Myself Through: Peace
A state of calmness; freedom from disturbance

For me, peace means to be void of loud sounds of the city. It is your family and daily life commitments. Peace is the present goal brought on by past life experiences. It is given freely, put in chains not to be claimed until the grave.

From the time I walked into the church at the young age of five, I wanted the calmness, the happiness and rest that reigned on her. She never looked her age (over 60) but glowed like a newborn sun. She smelled like baby powder and early morning freshness, which made you think of lavender. She would place me on my seat and say, "wait here," while she did the communion setting humming her favorite song. I would marvel at her smile thinking she had no problems. How does she get pass life troubles, struggles and bad meanings, I'd often wonder. I set thinking if she was real or just a ghost floating on this planet. I knew she was a grown woman, fully dressed having conversations with me, but her peace mimicked those that had passed on.

How have the cares of life threatened to overtake you in your internal and external body? Do you dwell in fear and anxiety on a daily basis? Do you ache for a good night's sleep? When has your life carried a grey cloud of turmoil and distress over you? Did you know true peace can be found and implemented in your daily life?

Psalm 119:105 states, "Thy word is a lamp unto my feet, and a light unto my path." Just as the daylight shines in a house for many hours of the day, God's word brings light, encouragement, and peace to any situation. As you read these passages, allow the living word of God to be a light to your path, to the peace that surpasses all understandings. I will not have to go the grave to have it!

I started with a reflection of peace from my childhood when I was with my grandmother at church. I was very blessed to have both grandmothers at this time of my life and they were able to clearly demonstrate and define peace for me. My mother's mother is the grandmother I spoke of; she knew the world we lived in. The media plagues us with pictures, stories, and words of wars, earthquakes, floods, rapes, murders and other calamities. We also can note the opposite of man's great knowledge, wealth and luxurious lifestyle that also need peace active as they live through this time.

We think (or thought) all the new modern technological advances would save us time and bring peace, but our lives are just as complicated to keep these things evident to do the task it was meant to do to make our lives easier. The provision for us to have peace lies in Romans 5:1, "Therefore being justified by faith, we have peace with and through our Lord Jesus Christ." Thinking of how God loved us so much that he sent His one and only beloved Son Jesus Christ to redeem and restore mankind; so, evidence states peace begins with Him. Peace is provided and established by the Prince of peace. We must accept Jesus Christ as Lord and Savior in order to experience true peace. Sadly, and due to lack of knowledge, people today who have accepted Jesus Christ still suffer and have not grasped the concept of peace. This is because they have not accepted him as the peace giver.

It is often stated that we are greedy, walking with spirits of entitlement, not counting our blessings. Being grateful for all you have, all you do, and all who benefit from your fruits is a key component to the peace life. However, when your motives are impure, and your sole focus is accumulating accolades, achievements that are not purposeful, or material possessions, it will be impossible to find peace. The creepy theory and implementation always bring about the consumption of more. We are not the best predictors of what will bring lasting peace. You can find yourself in an unrelentless pursuit of peace and never understand that may not have it.

In our jobs, home life and community, it is said, "develop a growth mindset". This is the power of believing you can improve and shift your mind into a state of ongoing growth; establishing the root of not being intimidated by the idea that your abilities are not currently as great as you would like. The mind constantly changes almost in sync with our emotions, so those abilities are not set in stone. They can change even to implement something as great as peace.

Growth Mindset is called by God in these scriptures: "Do not conform to the pattern of this world but be transformed by the renewing of your mind." (Romans 12:2). "With God, all things are possible." (Matthew 19:26). "To him who is able to do immeasurably more than all we ask or imagine, according to his power that is at work within us." (Ephesian 3:20).

What's the biggest reason peace is not consistent, sustainable or implemented with a growth mindset? What reasons are you making out to be excuses and in turn sabotaging your peace? Is it a lack of real organized time? Is it a lack of money? Is it a person or group always stalking, tearing down or making you feel you unworthy?

Peace Success/Failure

How do you define peace success and failure? Will you be peaceful when you get a certain title, job or amount of money? Will you be peaceful when you build the perfect marriage, have a baby and a big house to live in? The truth is that peace looks different for everyone. Those who chase peace based on how it fits into this life existence of things rarely attain it. Peace success can't be defined by earthly possessions. We can't serve two masters because we will love one and hate the other. Value peace fulfillment more than success. Aim for excellence, not short-lived success.

In what ways are you focused on getting to the peace goal line? Do nothing but your best to get there. Measure your peace by God's standards and not the world's. Ask yourself, "Is peace making me a better person, better Christian, putting me in a growth mindset? Does it allow me to release the negative?

Build Your Peace Muscles

We need peace, which helps build self-control and spiritual control. Self-control is the ability to resist temptation or embrace that which will move you in the right direction. Peace combined with self-control is a great discipline. It is consistent and will help with perseverance in the peace realm. It is about setting, implementing, evaluating and maintaining the peace goal through all obstacles, trials and tribulations.

In what area of life will you combine both peace and self-control as one unit? What area in your peace plan can benefit from the action of peace and self-control? What peace level added to self-control would you have to exhibit in order to conquer those potential distraction that causes loss of self-control?

Consider a pivotal moment in your life when you had to dig deep to the core of your being to unearth peace, self-control and spiritual control. What obstacles most threaten your peace (internally and externally)? Which peace strategy will most support or help you conquer and equate the obstacle and/or threat to peace sustainability?

Start with the area that needs the most peace. Choose and be engaged to pursue the peace. Target your productive and implementation plan. Peace is not the goal of everyone, but there are people with the same desire to have peace, and not just in short phases, but life abundantly. The coaching community will encourage the creation of a vision board but replace it with a peace board. Expect a challenge and determine the steps forward and those that will count you back.

Examine the ways in which peace can build peaceful emotions. The social well-being: this area synthesizes our close relationships. Ask yourself, as it pertains to my relationships, are they qualitative or quantitative? What needs to be repaired or released?

Professionally, choose a lifestyle that gives challenges, growth mindset and the money to promote your peace plan. Physically: place the peace plan in front of you, tag it on your phone, think of the peace place, where you can have moments of calmness and meditation.

As for the community well-being: is peace visible, active and able to transcend to others? Peace is connecting to others that can absorb it. The spiritual well-being includes all the ways of God that can help, guide and wash the soul. Only He can make peace sustainable, build capacity and stay actively engaged.

You don't have to be a certain age to have lose peace. I have been working on my peace as of today for forty-two years. I lost it when I was twelve years old. My mother and father both became ill. I had a sister who had been on drugs for fourteen years. I was 21 when my brother was murdered (he was only 22 years old). I lost all four of my grandparents in a month's time. I have had countless trips to the hospital for my parents. I was hospitalized at the age of 35 with the possibility of cancer (thank God for his healing). I was diagnosed at 45 with a tumor in my breast that through prayer was not cancerous.

I work for Chicago Public Schools; this year will mark 25 years as a Learning Behavior Specialist at the elementary level. I wondered why I've had so many trials and tribulations in my life? Had I offended God? I was at the highest levels of stress, feeling abandoned and some days full of despair.

I have wondered about the body of Christ and my own body when we speak of Jesus being the peace that passes all understanding. I often wondered if my peace was only found in the church? Why could it not transform or transfer itself to my everyday living? We adore and praise God, but we don't understand that the true purpose is to know "In his Name all things are possible".

It is not easy to talk about peace without the connection to God because they are one in the same. There is peace in you and in His name when combined and balanced. Mark 16:18 reads, "They shall lay hands on the sick, and they shall recover." To be without peace is to walk in sickness. Acts 3:6 states, "Such as I have given thee in the name of Jesus Christ of Nazareth rise up and walk." Peace belongs to every believer. It's a privilege for us to have this wonderful connection to remind us that stress, sickness and disease don't belong in our bodies.

What Do Your Thoughts Say?

I have heard many speakers, coaches and even older family speak about the mind. How it can be a destructive force and/or growth source. We allow our thoughts to control of us in positive and negative ways. The key to living a peaceful life is guarding our minds and our thoughts. What we think and do requires us to take control of the outcome of how we react to the various thoughts we engage in. Our thoughts are plagued by outside forces, which can create illusions, delusions and false peace. Bringing peace to the entire body begins with the mind; we must get control of our default mindset.

Thoughts that do not reflect peace are often plagued with fear and torment and gives place to the devil. It is important that we never allow our thought patterns to engage in non-peace interaction. A weak conceptual view doesn't give inspiration of peace and all it can offer us. I think of the number of years invested in seeking my peace. Peace is worth having and can be part of you daily. Women anticipate unhappiness on a large scale in comparison to their male counterparts. Women anticipate trials and tribulations and prepare for most of them in such a way that they can overcome or avoid them. When this happens, most time we give up our peace to make the situation comfortable for others. We are always putting ourselves last. At some point, you must ask yourself, "Am I making decisions in my life that promote peace?"

Peace Coaching

I often ask myself, "In what ways have I embraced a growth mindset, knowing and believing in my peace plan and vision? What areas of the plan can be set in stone and cannot be improved upon?" I have found myself at the beginning of every New Year making decisions about my relationships with family, friends, coworkers and new relationships. It is important to evaluate each of them to know which ones will help the development and implementation of the peace plan. This is a difficult process because of the elimination of some of the relationships in each area group.

I wonder about the goal of peace and how I have wanted to reach it for some time. I am on that journey and each day I love the challenge. When I need to be at peace for a task, I reflect on myself, God's life plan for me, and how those around me are affected, infected and effected by my peace. What can I do to eliminate, remove, minimize and maximize that which tempts or distracts my peace in any situation? What strategies guarantee my success with the peace implementation and elimination of it? If I could have a conversation with God in this moment, in what way do I want Him to present His plan of peace for me?

Critique yourself. What do you expect peace to do? What does it look like? Does it have sustainability and room for growth? Do you genuinely want it and the work to put into it? What can you do about the lack of discipline you have in maintaining your vision in each area?

Becoming Valorie

I have found after writing six books that your thoughts and thought processes can't be held hostage within your mind. Writing and implementation of anything doesn't just happen because your brain is full of great ideas; it is giving those ideas homes so new buildings can be built. Words are powerful and when we put them in written expression, they become insight to lead to the road to clarity. They become leaders, bosses and even coaching concepts. They become peace and happiness that bring excitement, a form of gratitude, great possibilities and move the vision and mission to the next levels. It reflects one's life of calmness and relief of how life can be better when that peace and/or person with peace has made a life better when they cross paths.

Understand that peace is not something that is here today and gone tomorrow. John 14:27 reads, "I am leaving you with a gift peace of mind and heart. And the peace I give is a gift the world cannot give. So, don't be troubled or afraid." According to this verse it is noticeably clear that peace is structured to transcend; its usage and existence connects to lifelong transcending powers.

Peace is strong and built to deal with every relationship in your life from your parents, siblings, friends, and foes. How do we begin to cultivate peace that no longer need people as the determining factor? I come back to the same pursuing behavior: to have peace it is a deliberate and much needed choice. I thrive to have it with my relationships, and completing the goals set forth in my life. I was once thinking, what if my peace says you must release people from your life? Now, I can do this. I had to weigh the pros and cons of my relationships. I had to understand that life is not perfect but all that happens is not in my control.

When making decisions about relationships (to keep or release them), I am very sure and fair when I walk away. Maya Angelou once said, "If people show you who they are believe them". I am now 52 years old and have found this to be true. It's not our job to change people; we can let them know what we are willing to do and going to deal with. If a relationship is keeping you in a constant state of stress, one-sided with a lack of growth, you have to decide why keep it. Life is not fair, but God is just. He will work things out if we will trust him.

Peace is the one thing that can make you reflect on times in your life when you transcended it. It comes at a time when trials and tribulations are so unbearable. You must go to a time and place that allows the body and mind to become one. If you are a person that believes in God, be at peace with him, know him and pursue him. If you are not a person that believes or have not developed the esteem to believe in yourself, be at peace. If you have poor relationships, begin to be at peace and make sure you are working on relationships that will promote the peace plan.

Now is the time to let go of things we can't change. Rise to maintain a life of quietness and inner self-reflection. When engaging in relationship with others, set boundaries, meet their needs within the peace boundaries, don't engage in negativity, be truthful with them and yourself, and above all aggressively pursue peace with yourself and with God. Releasing trials and tribulation is important, but the true pursuit is peace. Conversations with God are to develop your peace plan. Psalms 31:14-15 says, "O Lord: I said you are my God and my times are in your hand." God thrives greatest when we give Him our worries; and when we do this, it brings perfect peace. The way we humble ourselves is the balance. This balance says that we don't have to figure it out alone. We are to release the tears and fears and know that victory is in the plan.

I spoke a lot about God being my peace coach, advisor and savior because in my life they are not separate entities. God needs to be your partner in everything you say and do if you are to be successful in your peace journey. I have so many things going on in my life and they were not the barriers of peace, but of destruction. With the trials and tribulations that drained my energy, joy, and sustainability, I never thought peace could be achieved. However, when I begin to give over to God my wants, desires, and goals, I attained peace. God and I became partners; he energizes me by grace, restores my soul, hears my cries, consoles my soul. If my priorities get out of order, I know I will labor in vain and tire quickly. That is when I realize I am not partnering with God and must stop, reflect, and coach myself back to peace.

Peace

Lord, Lead the Way: Longsuffering

*Having or showing patience
in spite of troubles, especially those
caused by other people*

Just made 38 and I am finding myself still being a mother of 3. Upon hearing that one may say, "You should not have had the kids if you did not want take on the responsibility". But you see this was not the case for me because what I thought would be temporary has turned into a lifetime.

About five years ago, I had the perfect life. I had no kids, a full-time job and was going to school full-time. I had no one to answer to but myself and I was also still living with my mom; this allowed me to travel at least four times a year. However, in December 2013, my life would take a drastic shift.

My mom called and told me to check on my sister Lisha when I got out of church. I asked what was going on because I'd just seen her two days ago. Mom said, "I think she is getting back suicidal". I couldn't believe it and reassured her that I would go. Later that day, I went to her house and my sister was not sounding good at all. As the evening approached, I decided to spend the night just to make sure that things would stay safe for her and her three kids.

Around ten o'clock, my niece Lisha (named after her mom), came running in the room saying, "My mom just told me to jump off the porch". As she was telling me this, my sister walked in with the craziest look I had ever seen. I had to think quick, so to calm both of them down I told my niece to take deep breaths. I told my sister to go to the porch and allow me to talk to Lisha. Thank God it worked because when she left the room, I called 911 and she was put in the hospital. A week later, they released her saying that she was fine. I told them my sister was very clever and knew how to work the system.

At this point, DCFS was not notified because there was no immediate danger to the children, but I did not want those kids to go back home to her, so me and my other sister tag teamed. Me, my niece and nephews stayed at her house for about a week. That Saturday, it became clear that my sister Lisha would not be able to care for herself, let alone her children. It was late in the evening when she said that she was ready to go home; her daughter didn't want to go, but her boys did, so against my better judgement, I allowed them to walk out the door with their mom.

About two hours, later my nephew Nate called me

and said their house was on fire. My older sister and her son rushed to the house while I called 911. By the time I made it, my sister Lisha was in handcuffs and my other sister and two nephews were in the ambulance. Apparently, my sister had barricaded the back door with the refrigerator, so my nephew had to fight with her to get through the front door in order to let everyone in. While my nephew opening the door, she poured bleach on all of them. DCFS was called and the kids were ordered to stay at our house temporarily. Within a month, a DCFS counselor came to the house and stated one of us would have to take custody of the kids or they would be taken into custody.

I gladly stepped up not knowing or understanding what I was signing up for. I just knew at that time I did not want them to be separated. I tell everyone that my getting custody of my sister's kids almost resembles Bernie Mac's story when he had to get custody of his sister's kids because she was on drugs. The ages for his kids were 2, 4 and 6 while my kids were 13, 15, and 18.

When I first got custody of the kids, my family told me they would help me. As time went on, I found myself alone and frustrated sort of how Bernie Mac felt when he was in the courtroom, leaned back and saw that his brother had left him to take full custody. Although it doesn't sound like it, the three people who are currently in my house have change my life the better. Oftentimes, I hear people say I saved those kids, but I turn around and say, "No, those kids saved me."

I will start with princess Lisha; she is growing up to be a queen. Lisha was 13 when I got her and now, she is almost 18 and a senior at Von Steuben. When I first got her, she was in eighth grade and was extremely behind because she was barely going to school. So, when I got custody of her, I had to establish a middle ground because I viewed education as important and not to be taken lightly. The same rules applied as it pertained to doing chores and having a curfew. I was very frustrated as I couldn't understand how I and my sister grew up in the same household, yet she gave her children no rules whatsoever. Although my niece didn't like the rules initially, as time went on, she got used to them.

I taught her the importance of taking care of herself financially and she got her first job with After School Matters. I showed her how to use public transportation so that she could travel to school, work etc. I also made time to talk with her throughout the week about her experiences; she was able to spend time with both her dad and mom at least twice a month. I noticed that even though she was hurt from the situation, she still longed to have a relationship with them, and I didn't want to deny her.

In the beginning, it worked fine, but then as time

went on both of her parents became very isolated and did not want to be bothered not understanding how they were breaking her heart. Day by day, month by month I would tell them she needed them, but they ignored me repeatedly. On top of that, she was being bullied at school, so she started overeating and gained 50 pounds by the time she was a sophomore in high school.

She was very sad and depressed, so I got her into counseling; upon seeing her, they wanted to put her on medication. I refused because I did not want history to repeat itself. My brother was put on medication when he was 16 and now at 32 years old, he can't do anything for himself.

Lisha had begun to change. She did not want to take a proper bath, did not want to clean up and only wanted to go outside, but not to school. She started ditching school, either leaving early or not going on Fridays because she'd claim she was sick. Within months, she started having panic attacks, which took her away from school for about a month. Through a series of test, it was realized that Lisha might be bipolar like her mother, which was the last thing I wanted to hear or have to deal with.

A few months later, I found out that my niece was considering being with another woman. I told her I would still love her, and God would too, but homosexuality is a sin before God that comes with deadly consequences. I would know because I almost had my own deadly experience when I was thinking about being a lesbian. So I encouraged my niece to talk about it. I wanted her to go back to counseling, but she refused. She said she did not need any help and all she needed to do was draw when she got frustrated, depressed, sad, etc.

I realized that my niece was in denial, but I was caught between a rock and a hard place. I knew she needed more help than drawing, but the way it works when it comes to mental health, until they endanger themselves or another person nothing can be done. Little did I know a week later, my niece would be hospitalized for a suicide attempt! I was so grateful to God because I could have been at work and this situation could have gone completely different. However, since I was there, I was able to stop things before they got out of hand. Today, my niece is doing fine. She is going to counseling and is taking her medicine. Thank you, Jesus!

My nephew, Robert is 20 years old; but when I got custody of him, he was 15 and was attending Jones College Prep. I knew that Robert received Social Security, but I did not know why. When I got custody, I had to go to Social Security and become the representative payee for both he and his brother, Nate. As time went on, I found out that Robert did not know how to read, but I could do nothing about it because I was working two jobs 15 hours a day. About two years later, when I stopped working one of the jobs, I put my focus back on its original purpose and that was the kids.

I decided to investigate the Special Ed program that was being given at Jones College Prep. I was not happy because I didn't understand why my nephew was about to be a junior but did not know how to read. Jones is rated as one of the top schools in Chicago, so I was shocked to see this program didn't benefit the disabled. That year, I decided to transfer Robert to Al Raby because of the reviews and the fact that they had a job program inside the school that specialized in helping youth with disabilities. Although I believed this to be a good choice, I learned that I was wrong. Unbeknownst to me, Robert's girlfriend attended this school which caused a lot of other problems I was not prepared to handle.

When I first got custody of him, the only thing I knew was they were good friends. I had no idea that Robert was very obsessed with this girl and wanted a relationship. Within six months, of them attending school they started having sex and there was a possibility that she was pregnant. Thank God that the test was negative because neither one of them were in a position to take care of a baby.

As time went on, the relationship became very unhealthy because they were having sex in school and Robert started engaging in several fights with different boys because of jealously. He had several suspensions and was forced to separate from his girlfriend while in school. This is when Robert's temper got worse and he started hitting the walls at home. I told him that behavior wouldn't be tolerated. I told him he needed to find a constructive way to deal with his anger and frustration. I suggested he go to the gym and punch a bag.

I also told him that he would have to accept the truth and stop being in denial. Using shows like 'Snapped' or 'First 48' as examples, I explained how jealousy could go wrong; people who snapped and killed somebody or killed themselves because of it. But it went in one ear and out the other. Although he feels I can't relate to what he was going through, I explained that he was making some of the same mistakes I'd made.

Despite the fact that this bad situation got started because of the transfer it was not all in vain. Robert was able to get in the job training program and is now working at both Jewel and Soldier Field. Overall, I am so excited for Robert's growth because I can honestly say the experience helped him mature. His older brother, Nate, is a different story.

At the age of 23, Nate has a lot of growing up to do. One day, he wants to play with action figures and books, but then the next day wants to be treated like a grown man. It is an ongoing battle because I am trying to get him to understand that he is now an adult and cannot keep on switching back and forth from childhood to adulthood depending on the day. I told him I refused to take care of a grown boy. It was time to grow up, I explained, so that once he turned 30, he'd be a man of God and ready for the world.

As I look back, when I first got Nate, he was 18 years old and apparently had just had his first sexual encounter. He told me this about a month ago when we were talking about sex. But when I got custody of him, he also received Social Security, which I did not understand, but soon found out. Apparently, Nate not only had an intellectual disability, but it also suffered from Obsessive Compulsive Disorder. If you are not familiar, basically once my nephew gets something or someone fixated in his brain, he will not let it go until it manifests. No matter how wrong it may seem to us in his brain it seems to be the best choice in life.

Case in point, he was trying to date this girl online, of which I didn't approve. This girl was telling him that she was coming to Chicago but never showed up which made him very frustrated; this caused him to pick on his sister. No matter what I said, he still wanted to be with this girl – even insisted on seeing her on his birthday.

Despite it all, Nate has grown as well but in a special way. After all, he is one of the reasons why he, his brother and mom are still alive. He is the one that had to fight with his mom to get the door open for the police and family. He is the one that sneakily got the phone out of my sister's hand in order to call me and let me know they were in trouble. Nate is also the one that went through a horrific, police beating.

As I look at Nate's academic and work record, it is very different from Robert's even though they both have the same intellectual disability. Nate knows how to read I would say at a fifth-grade level and he graduated from Ray Gram Training Center, a school for the disabled. He also has completed one year of college and is about to start his next term. As far as working, he will start with the Chicago Park district.

Having all three of them has been quite amazing. Despite all of what we are going through and the things that are coming, I still give God the praise. You know God has made it clear to me in this season that I need to lean on Him by casting all my cares upon him and not being anxious for nothing. The Bible says in Psalm 138 that the Lord will perfect that which concerneth me. I live by this scripture because daily these three are getting into something that will not benefit their future. I say to the Lord, "Daily you are the same God from 20 years ago when I was a teenager and was refusing counsel and lord I am asking and believing that the same way you did me, you would do them but sooner than later."

The Lord has brought us through some tremendous hurdles. We are still working on (and have not conquered) the importance of praying. They often tell me they are not saved so they should not have to pray, and I tell them that one day you will have to decide who you will serve. The goal of the praying is for you to gain an intimate experience with God so that when you make your decision it should be an easy choice.

Before or after we pray, I do a separate prayer, in which I ask God for clarity and wisdom on what I should be doing for them. I ask God to reveal their purpose so that I can encourage them on the importance of taking care of His will rather than their will. This is so I don't waste time getting them into some program that will not fit their future or their purpose. I ask questions like what job would be best for them considering they all have their different challenges that they are currently facing as they become mature adults. I ask God for guidance in every area of life because I do not have time to waste. I have suffered enough and am ready to move on with what God's will is for my life and my young adults.

Revenge is Never Sweet: Gentleness

The quality of being kind, tender, or mild-mannered

Valeria was a married woman. She married when she was young and thought she had married for love. Little did she know there was a whole lot more to life than she thought.

She divorced young; she married because her parents put it in her head that at 18, she was grown and on her own. So, at that point, marriage was a crutch for her.

Valeria was on her second marriage in less than nine months. She did not give herself time to heal; she jumped right into a new relationship. She refused to give up on her second husband. This time, she was in it for the long run no matter what. Life was grand, or so she thought.

She was married, had a job, her husband had a job, and now they had a child together – just what she'd expected.

Valeria and her husband moved into an apartment building in a close-knit neighborhood; she did not socialize too much although her husband did. She knew most of the people in the building; her husband grew up with most of them.

Valeria was quiet. She did not interact with many people; she most stayed to herself.

Valeria grew up in an abusive home as an only child. Her father would beat her mother as his father did to his mother. So, she was always quiet. She did not talk much because she did not want people in her business. Her father was very abusive to her mother, so there was not too much of a conversation in the home. When he was happy times were good; when he was not so happy, times were bad.

She had sworn to herself that she would never let a man treat her the way that her father treated her mother.

One day, Valeria came home only to find that she was not the only woman in her husband's life. This triggered an emotional set back because she had seen so much of this same display from her uncles and its effect on their wives.

This was a life changing moment for her, as you can imagine. There were things said and done as a result of her husband's actions; however, she did not give up on him, they stayed together.

One morning Valeria got up for work. Her husband lay still in the bed. She began to ponder on the life they had together. She began to think about those that had given her advice on marriage and how they thought it should be.

She began to realize that their opinions were not her business, but what she did not consider was the cause and effect of her jumping into another relationship. She had her view of what life was supposed to be and she did not need their approval. She had forgiven him, but there was still particles and residue. It made her wonder, if this is the first time he got caught, how many times had this happened before?

This was a new bright sunny day and she decided to go to work and not allow her thoughts to deter or detour her. On her way to work, a man stopped her in the hallway of the building where she lived. He looked familiar, but she was not sure. He started flirting and smiling at her. She was not sure what brought that on, but it made her feel some kind of way; it felt good to know that she was still attractive to someone else. She thought nothing of the encounter and went on with her daily routine.

That Saturday, she was having some alone time and enjoying it. She did not work on weekends, but her husband did; their child was with relatives. She was at home relaxing not expecting any company. There was a knock at the door. She knew it had to be someone in the building because visitors had to ring the bell.

She opened the door to a face that seemed familiar. The guy introduced himself as James. He told her how he and her husband had many conversations about her, so he felt as if knew her. At this point, they were enjoying each other's company. He invited her to come to his apartment and she accepted the invitation.

Sometime later, Valeria found out she was pregnant. She was in a dilemma because she did not know who the father was – her husband or her neighbor, James. So, she told them both that she was pregnant. Her neighbor had just gotten married but was still keeping company with Valeria. They were both married with children but could not stop seeing each other. There was a bond between the two of them that could not be broken.

Three years later, the neighbor's wife had another child and they needed more room, so they moved, but only a couple blocks away. They continued seeing each other, but Valeria had come to the point where she wanted to end their relationship and continue her life with her husband. James did not want the relationship to end because he loved her. The more she pulled away, the more he stalked her. He would wait for her in the driveway, then visit her job. He knew her routine, so he knew where to find her.

Valeria and her husband finally moved out of the neighborhood, as her job relocated somewhere else. Five years passed. She had not heard from him. From out of nowhere, she had a visitor at her job. She went to greet him; it was James. She explained she did not want to continue with the relationship.

She went on with life. She was still with her husband despite their infidelities. Her husband continued in his mess and she knew it, but she was not willing to let him go. Valeria had moved on. She was content; life was good with her and her family.

Fifteen years later, her husband was talking to one of his friends on the phone and she overheard the conversation. It was James. She learned that his mother had passed away; since her husband was well acquainted with the family, they went to the funeral.

Valeria returned home only to have a little remorse because she did not say anything to James at the funeral. She called his job to give him her condolences. He asked her to meet him at his job and she agreed. The two picked up where they had left off – only this time she was meeting him at hotels. The relationship was very intense because now they were both having a difference of opinion with their spouses. The love was lost with them, they had outgrown the relationships that they were never fully in. The bond that she and James had was so intense.

They both continued in their marriage and their daily routine but found time to do things together away from their spouses. She was well-established and he was living a good life also, but they could not let each other go. She tried, but he threatened her, so she continued seeing him.

One day she was supposed to meet him. They had made plans, but he did not show. She knew something was wrong because he never dismissed her. He never showed up for the meeting. She called him at work, but he wasn't there. She called his home and when the wife answered, she hung up. She drove past his house. The car was sitting with a flat tire and it was dirty; she knew something was wrong. He always kept his car clean. She had become the stalker. Months had passed and she did not hear from him.

One morning she overheard her husband talking on the phone. She was eavesdropping so she only heard her husband's words. James had died of cancer. She then knew why he did not meet her; he'd become ill. Her neighbor, her friend and lover had died.

Gentleness is a strong slap with a soft touch. It is a tender and compassionate and considered way to act towards others' feebleness and limitations. A gentle person will sometimes tell the truth even when it is painful.

It's the sturdy hand, not the frail one, that must learn to be gentle.

The heart speaks with common sense and if we are not careful the mind will rationalize our desires and reactions and sometimes cause us to make the wrong decisions. The heart and mind battle to decide between how your mind might sound verses what your heart is saying. We battle every day with our heart's desires compared to what we think. When our heart speaks to us, it takes courage to follow through on what it says – even if our mind protests. This is because we are human, and these things happen in life; no one is perfect or exempt.

The heart is the seat of all actions of life. It is the part of our being where we desire and decide. The place of consciousness, spiritual activity, feelings, desires, passions, thought, understanding and will.

We cannot change our past, but the decisions we make today can set the course for the future.

Sometimes we get caught up in our feelings and emotions and tend to ignore the cause and distress it causes from our actions and how it can create a stronghold in our lives.

From birth, we form a bond with our parents, siblings or someone that has for cared for us, whether it be good or evil. This sets the pace for us in our lives as we get older; we look for that love connection, good or bad, that we had as a child.

Love is the most powerful motive for almost everything we do; however, it can create emotions that bring on a hate to love your situation. Whatever feelings or motives we have that stem from love can cause a lot of emotions in our mind (good or bad). Yet, we need love like we need oxygen.

Gentleness is merciful, forgiving, compassionate, kind-hearted and good-natured.

Love causes us to be gentle, and when being gentle, we are merciful, compassionate and forgiving. Love can cause us to be strong and enable us to face whatever obstacle we must face.

Hate is an intense dislike or a hostile feeling. It comes and destroys our strength; it makes us weak. Hate causes us to make wrong decisions; it causes us to be bitter, foolish and regretful. Hate produces wrongful actions and anger; it never makes anything better.

Gentleness causes us not to rush to quick decisions. We have patience in whatever we are dealing with. An approach that gives us to understand that everyone fails at something; we are not perfect.

In life, there is a recipe for each dish. If the wrong ingredient is used in the mixture, the dish is spoiled or ruined and won't taste too good. How do we love someone when they have wronged us?

How can we heal if we won't take off the bandage? When we have been wounded from past experiences, from things that were said or done, we don't stop to think about the width or depths of our actions and the things we speak. The karma keeps giving devastating results from the past wounds leaving us numb.

The actions that were received from previous relationships leaves us in an altered state. Because of the things we hear and see, the experience we have gone through affects how we feel, and an action causes a reaction whether positive of negative.

A positive and a positive, puts us on the same page; a negative and a positive means someone must walk away. If there are two negatives, it causes death emotionally and sometimes physically.

When we are emotionally scarred, our mind and heart suffer. Those scars effect our thoughts and our character because we look back at the past, and the recording of all the negative film keeps replaying like an old movie.

We begin to restore the broken fragmented pieces that have been damaged and carry them over into the next relationship. We can't give ourselves wholeheartedly because we keep replaying what happened and how it happened, and we remain vulnerable and captive to the past.

Some of us have accepted fake emotions in our minds. They have been deposited and we hold on to them; they never come out. When the positive comes, we are so used to the negative that we can't receive the kind-hearted, gentle person presented before us. We reject them because the previous behavior has become a lifestyle.

When we are born, we are put on this earth for a reason. There is a purpose for our lives; we all have a destiny that we must fulfill. When we lean to our negative understanding of life, we are being selfish, and our lack of control leads to bondage. Revenge is a natural response to being injured. Whether it is an emotional or physical hurt, revenge leads to wrong. Sometimes we spend too much time thinking of ways to get back at whomever wronged us, and we suffer from unfulfilled potential and we never grow; we remain stagnant. This allows temptation to overtake us, as we are all tempted where we are most weak.

We all need love and the feeling of security, but if one has the wrong motives, emotional dependency becomes a problem because now the bond becomes defined by those needs. We are now in bondage and enslaved to each other. The end results are control and manipulation.

One is in bondage and the other is the feeder. The feeder feeds the one in bondage with flattery, financial and material things, never allowing the other to be around others. They keep you alone by expressing dislike of your friends and family, wanting to keep you to themselves. The one in bondage has an emotional dependency with the other person. They have no interest in others, just that one person. Jealousy, envy following or stalking – they get aroused even when the feeder is not around.

When the feeder is not around, the one in bondage feels alone. They have been manipulated; loneliness, insecurity, low self-esteem, fear and rebellion become part of their destiny because of these emotional scars. Those scars show up repeatedly in each relationship for fear of being rejected.

When someone has gotten into our emotional closet, they have captured us. We long for each other's spirit and become one. Sometimes in relationships it is hard to sever the emotional cord. It becomes a bond no matter how detrimental it is to us.

In life, when we see food if it looks good, we desire it. We eat it, and the food becomes part of us. Even when we have a bowel movement, the particles remain. There is no gentleness in deceit or revenge.

Is It Ever Enough: Goodness

The quality of being kind, tender, or mild-mannered

✿ ✿ ✿ ✿ ✿ ✿ ✿ ✿

Do you have to feel good to be a blessing to others?

"You don't have to feel good to bless people. The more you get your mind off you, the happier and freer you will be."

When I saw this reflection point in my fruit of the spirit action plan journal by Joyce Meyer I said, "wow" to myself. It clearly defines goodness as a state of the heart, while kindness is the direct action or behavior that expresses the good within us. Do you think it's possible to be good and not be kind, or vice versa? I must see this through the eyes of being a follower of Christ. It's clear that we have been called to be God's heart and hands on earth. Being kind in our attitudes and doing well through our deeds for others who are not part of our normal family make up. We have no thought of the reward but only edifying the kingdom.

Think about your attitudes and behaviors toward others. Are you consistently kind, or consistently rude, or even consistently unable to filtrate your emotions and words with others? If you are not, where do you fall short?

Do you want to show kindness and goodness or are you content in what is going on with your cause and effect behaviors towards others?

What does it mean to put on love "on purpose"?

Why do actions speak so much louder than words?

Don't answer these questions all at once because goodness and kindness are an outgrowth of the Holy Spirit's gentle nudges in our lives. Can you think of a time when you felt the Holy Spirit or something you couldn't clearly identify nudging you to do something kind for someone? What was the result?

I am currently working on an action plan personal study guide called, Fruit of the Spirit: How to Water God's Word in Your Life and Relationships by Joyce Meyer. It assists me in balancing my everyday life with what kindness and goodness looks like — especially as we think and reflect on the causes and effects in our lives.

When thinking about the causes and effects of kindness and goodness it comes to a take-action situation. Being kind is a conscious, deliberate pursuit. The more kindness I implement, the more I desire to continue to meet the need to do them. For example, our church has a Community Meal Program that cooks hot meals once or twice a month depending on the goal of the committee that runs it. The meals or not hot dogs and soda; they are well thought out as if you are in a restaurant having lunch with families and friends. Our church members and some neighborhood volunteers run the meal. The church members provide funding for this meal program. I don't serve the food, but I do contribute a great deal of funds to support the purchase of food to be prepared for the community in which at times can feed up to three hundred people.

The goal is to think of small acts of kindness and goodness that you can contribute to on a level that will be consistent and sustainable to the life of the project. The acts of kindness and goodness can be performed today, tomorrow, next week, monthly, yearly to people you know or don't know.

The days are long and short depending on how you see the outcomes of your deeds and behaviors on a given day. When thinking about goodness and kindness, think of them in terms of quality and/or quantity. This not to determine if one is more desired or even greater than the other, but to determine how they balance in your life.

Think about how and why goodness and kindness are important in your life. It is important to go over it several times! Meditate on it. I sometimes think and ponder on what applies to me and what applies to the whole concept of kindness and goodness especially when applicable to the bible. I was taught in Sunday School, and Bible Study that before you hear or discuss the word, you must have made some decision that with God's implementation, strategies and patient help you do what the word says. When the opportunity presents itself, walk and work in kindness and goodness with self and others. Yes, with self because if you can't be kind to yourself it may be even more difficult to be kind to others.

If you struggle in many things, find one thing that stands out to you, or that quickens your heart that you really need to do when it comes to kindness and goodness. The first act of kindness is to family and neighbors because they surround us more than any other humans in the world on a daily, weekly, monthly and yearly basis. One thing that is evident about kindness and goodness is the ability to work and walk in time. Be clear about who and what you are that requires evaluation – especially to effectively deliver such a great fruit to others. I want to think and reflect on the goodness and kindness theory of being needed to help self and others. There are many ways to reflect, but not all can help you be good and kind on a consistent basis especially with life's trials and tribulations.

Goodness and kindness are forms of truth, and when we follow these two concepts, we are engulfed in free behaviors. Goodness and kindness are life, healing and a way to health in the spirit and heart. Goodness and kindness can help deliver us from the void of sadness and emptiness. They operate in the arena of wisdom, prosperity and success with self and others. They can help balance skills of stability, fruit building in your life, church and community. They can bring fulfillment in all we do to move from a default mindset to a growth mindset. It is awesome to know that goodness and kindness give the power to create. To know that organizations for education and faith-based ones are working together to better communicate about the presence of food and economic deserts. My own community of Englewood has been noted as both at one point, but with the kindness and goodness of grant writers and small business owners, we are growing back to a stable community.

Thinking and continuing my decision to help others, I think back to a quote by Charles Dickens: "No one is useless in this world who lightens the burdens of another." Our country has been built on wars and rumors of wars. It has supported charities inside and outside of its own boundaries. Think in turns of the history of the Salvation Army, which was founded in 1865. It still exists as a large and thriving institution that helps others. It was an over 150 years ago.

It was Christmas Eve, 1910. General William Booth, living in England was near the end of his life. It was noted his health was poor and he was going to be unable to attend the Army's annual convention. army of volunteers who would (and continues to) bring salvation to the poor that reside on the streets as well as hungry. The mission and vision of the Salvation Army is still carried out today in over 127 countries around the world. When looking back at my studies with Joyce Meyers' reading, I came across the history of the Salvation Army.

It states that General William Booth and his wife Catherine started The Salvation Army Basically, Booth had become an invalid, with failing eyesight. It was clear that there would not be another Christmas in his future. So, it was suggested that he send a message to the soldiers and volunteers that would be attending the event. When the thousands of delegates met, and the envelopes were opened to reveal his message it read: "OTHERS!" The call to serve and have a joy for serving others was clear. This is what goodness and kindness is about; there is no separating them.

I have written and experienced peace, but these are also the key components – to support peace and the profound joy that comes with goodness and kindness through the helping of others. According to Acts 20:35, "It is more blessed (makes one happier and more to be envied) to give than to receive." We often say, "I don't have anything to give", but that is not true no matter how desolate we may feel. When we are plagued with our own despair and anguish, we rarely feel like helping or showing kindness and goodness to others.

We have so many times asked ourselves, "if I am helping others through my kindness and goodness, well how does that really help me?" This questioning and thinking process needs an example and we can think back to Christmas, Mother's Day, Thanksgiving and other holidays. The joy of opening your gifts on these days as well as watching the anticipation of those receiving the gift brings about a wonderful and warmth of joy. The process and steps taken to find the right fit for the individual you have selected to be kind and good to on these specific days. Please note, it is not just these times you can bring kindness and goodness to others and reap the benefits of not only helping them but also helping yourself.

I think back to the summer of 2018. My mother wanted to do some redecorating to our family home. She wanted some new furniture, her house painted inside and out, new kitchen appliances, a table and new dining room set. I thought to myself, while that's a tall order, my mother is 82 years old and has been an awesome mother even to now. I have always been there for her and she has always been here for me, so this little request may be great in expense, but small to bring her joy, so it was not a problem.

My sister and I got together and divided the expenses and she enjoyed all her gifts from us. I was happy to give her that little request. I can see that goodness and kindness brought her happiness. It puts joy in my heart knowing that I was able to give her such a small gift because she has given so much to us already and continues to be there for us.

I don't want to give the impression that it is always easy to create or even give kindness and goodness, especially when we live in a world that promotes a great deal of strife among family, friends and foes. The world is clear about the goal to be on top, but the bible according to Matthew 20:16 states that the last will be first, and the first will be last. This is not to say you don't set goals but be careful how you are achieving those goals especially if you are not treating people with goodness and kindness.

Greed runs so rampant these days; companies robbing themselves, organizations robbing the poor and the misuse of funds to support those in need. The world operates in selfishness, stinginess, and greediness in order to have more than enough. The word of God according to Luke 6:38 says, "It will be given to you: good measure, pressed down, shaken together and running over."

Goodness and kindness cannot coexist with hating others, especially our enemies. We hold grudges, react with violence and speak in hurt to one another; this is not the way to walk in goodness and kindness. According to Matthew 5:44, God says, "love your enemies, and to pray for those who persecute you." Release it and walk in goodness and kindness. What is something you did that helped someone get through the day? Was it a word, deed, or activity? Don't feel that if you only care for yourself everything will be well; this is not healthy thinking. It is easy to be in the world for self, but the challenge comes when you go beyond.

According to Galatians 6:8, a man reaps what he sows, so sow goodness and kindness to reap goodness and kindness. Or, you can sow hate, distrust, selfishness and reap it. To sow into others is to live in a harvest greater than self and furnished by God.

I was reading a Sunday School lesson: Calling the Lost is to develop a heart for the lost like Jesus has. How in the world does the lost apply to goodness and kindness? "But the father said to his servants, 'Quickly, bring out the best robe and put it on him! Put a ring on his finger and sandals on his feet! Because this son of mine was dead and has come back to life! He was lost and is found!'" (Luke 15:22-24). I am going to reflect on a time in my life when my sister was the lost; I now thank God every day for her sobriety of 19 years.

She used drugs for 14 years and it was like a Six Flags Roller Coaster for my family during that time. We went through program after program to get her the needed help and one day I told my mother " I can't do it anymore. You must make a final decision concerning your child. I could not see beyond the addictive behavior. My mother decided to call Department of Children and Family Services.

When she contacted them, she made sure and was clear on letting them know that the help needed was for the mother and not the children. I was like the older child in the aforementioned scripture; I was working on myself and what I needed. I was working, going to school, taking care of my mother and was dealing with my own health concerns. We met with the DCFS workers, agents and went to court to determine the best course of action for this situation. My mother and I were given custody of the children. I was able to write and support a release plan for my sister that included 90 days of rehab, 2 years of court order outpatient treatment, parent planning to reengage with her children and psychological help to establish the root cause of her addiction.

When going through this process my sister was extremely mean to me and this is when the kindness and goodness manifested itself. I could have just beat her up, but that is not how you solve problems. I know some would say it really would have released some of the pressure, but my kindness and goodness needed to be more stable than a quick fight. That is when I knew that God had a plan for me and that I needed to know and operate in kindness and goodness. This required not only my finances and time, but also my love to my relatives in need.

I began to understand that these behaviors as an adult are not the true self. We engage in so many things that we forget what we looked like as children. Yes, we sometimes think back or have flashbacks. When we were children, my brother and sisters didn't physically fight each other, but as we became adults there has been some physical contact. How can this be when it was never part of the original upbringing? Family is so difficult to figure out, yet they reflect the people we would meet in the streets.

We know every family has a drug addict, a person struggling with sexual or gender identity, someone that has a low IQ, an alcoholic and an outcast. In the world where we find reflections and even clones in our daily lives that reflect the same behavioral structure of a family member, we show them kindness and goodness and not our own family. Is it because we don't have to take them home, or we may never see them again? Or because they will accept it better than that family member?

I find the older I get, the less I want to tolerate them and at times find myself isolating from them. I have met this with a sabbatical plan so I can reflect in a clear space what it is I need and why I feel this way. I use this time to make sure that the goodness and kindness can be evaluated and grow.

Embracing the New Normal: Humility

Low estimate of one's own importance; modest

Throughout my life, I've experienced things that caused me to adjust the way I'd grown accustomed or, as I like to say, "embrace a 'new normal'". Simply put, a "new normal" is a positive way of accepting change that must occur in your life – most times caused by events out of your control. It is the ability to embrace this adjustment that determines your level of humility, as the thought of a lifestyle change is often overwhelming for many.

One of the first times I had to embrace a "new normal" was when my mom died. For 22 years, I'd been used to calling my mother any time I had a problem. I never really had to figure anything out other than how to contact my mother. No matter the problem, she always seemed to have a solution. But once she died, I was left to figure things out on my own. Not seeing eye-to-eye with a family member? Couldn't call mom anymore to vent. If I was having relationship issues, I had to figure it out. Bouts with low self-esteem? That was my problem to solve. I actually had to be an adult and work things out on my own. And although that may seem very easy and straightforward, I suffered a lot along the way because I learned that I had more pride that I thought.

Before my mom died, if I had a problem with a family member, I'd reach out to mom and let her know and wait for her to work her magic. She'd either go and talk to the person for me or call us both to the table so we could talk it out and resolve the issue. No one was upset when Mom was involved; we just focused on the bigger picture of squashing our problems.

If I had relationship issues, I'd call her, tell her what happened and wait to hear what she had to say. She wasn't that mother to agree with me just because I was her child (one of the reasons I loved talking to her because I could always trust her to be fair). She would tell me when I was right as well as when I was wrong. And when I was wrong, she could advise me on how to fix the problem, so I didn't have to stay wrong.

But once she died, I had to figure out – on my own – when I was right and when I was wrong. This took me having to mature because the fact was, I very rarely thought I was wrong. I always thought myself to be reasonable and fair, so if my feelings were hurt, it just had to be the other person's fault, right? If only it were that simple!

After a while, I understood that I was wrong, but then I fell to the opposite extreme – I believed I was ALWAYS wrong. Every time anything went wrong in my relationship, I always found myself apologizing, whether or not I'd done something wrong. If he wasn't blaming me, I was blaming myself. I'd lost all sense of balance. It took time (and counseling) to get myself centered again. Once I did, I found myself wanting to release any relationship that brought negative energy to my life.

I learned that I'd actually had a few toxic ones that, because I wasn't centered, had gone unnoticed. So, now that I was committed to being a better person to and for myself, I had to make a conscious decision to let them go. And it wasn't easy, as this meant terminating relationships I'd had for years, and in some cases, decades.

Initially, it was awkward not having those people in my life. Some were completely cut off; some of the relationships were modified. My "new normal" meant that now I only allowed people in my life who would edify me. Please understand that for me, there is a difference between having "yes men" and being edified. Whereas I don't desire to be surrounded by people who will only tell me what I want to hear (yes men), I do want to have a circle who will tell me when I'm right and wrong. I need to have people who will give me the hard truths as a means of helping me grow; those who offer both constructive criticism and compliments.

One of the reasons that piece of the puzzle was so crucial for me was because I'd suffered with low self-esteem and struggled with depression and suicidal thought and tendencies for a very long time because of it. I never really trusted my own voice because it always told me how ugly and fat I was. That no one loved me. That I was a nobody. And it seemed the older I got, the louder that voice became. It didn't help that the people who I thought should have my best interest at heart; people who I depended on for validation, either turned their backs on me, didn't show up for me, or used the power I gave them against me. It just about ruined me.

In those days, I wasn't strong enough to deal with someone talking about me. I couldn't handle knowing that someone was mad at me. I compromised myself and my integrity too many times just so everybody else would like me. But little by little, I started identifying people who only seemed to like me as long as I was doing something for them. I could see people who really didn't care about my best interest.

So, I started taking back the power, position and priority I'd given them in my life. I decreased their voice and increased my own. I noticed that listening to myself wasn't so bad. In fact, it helped me to gain more confidence. That caused me to start liking myself. And over time, like turned into love – unconditional love. So that regardless of what size clothes I wore, I still believed myself to be beautiful. Regardless of my employment or relationship statuses, I knew I would be okay.

I truly embraced my "new normal". The one that said, "You may not have a house full of people, but as long as you love your own company, you'll be okay. Your social media posts and videos may not go viral, but as long as you stay true to yourself and help encourage or inspire somebody, you've done what you were supposed to do."

Embracing my "new normal" gave me permission to make mistakes – and be okay. To know that I don't have all the answers (and I never will), but I should always be willing to learn. Life may not be what you thought it was going to be, but as long as you are willing to adjust to what comes your way, to embrace your "new normal" you'll be just fine. I would not have naturally chosen the series of events that led me here, but I'm so glad that I've found myself here.

Keeping It Together:
Discipline
Training oneself to do something in a controlled and habitual way

I remember it as though it was yesterday. I found myself being sexually abused by a relative. At that point and time, I did not think it was anything wrong with what was going on. The fact of the matter is I thought it was normal; this is why it is so important to talk to your kids early.

I didn't tell a soul and as time went on, because of this abuse, I found myself having romantic feelings toward women. Since this lifestyle was not accepted nor tolerated by my family, I just decided to keep it to myself. Little did I know keeping it to myself would do more harm than good. I found myself watching porn and fantasizing over all the female high school teachers, which was my way of dealing with this situation until I turned 18.

At age 18, I had my first boyfriend; I was so love with this man. Unfortunately, I found out sometime later that he only wanted sex and not a relationship, which left me depressed and brokenhearted. I mean this man did not want to spend any time with me in public. I was still battling with perverted feelings, so I continued to watch porn as a way of coping with my sexuality.

But in 1999, I was approached by not one, but two women. I had just started working this new job and I noticed these two women giving me a look that said "interested". One day as I was getting dressed in the locker room, they approached me. I found out that they were lovers and only wanted to "hookup". I told them no because inside my soul I knew my family would not be okay with this lifestyle; little did I know this was God intervening. Looking back, God was all over this situation because even though I did not know of God then, I knew how important my family was and I did not want to disappoint them. So, God worked through my family. Therefore, I was able to stay on the straight and narrow path while I was growing into adulthood.

I decided to give dating another try only to meet up with a man who just wanted sex. After that, I took a break from dating for a couple of years. I later met the guy of my dreams, or at least that's what I thought. I met him through a non-for-profit organization where I was volunteering. We would often flirt with one another, but nothing was ever official; this went on for some years.

One day, the company was invited to a banquet and

Discipline

that's when I found out he was very involved with another woman. As you can probably imagine, I was in love, obsessed, and frustrated to say the least. I couldn't believe it. How could I have not known? Why could I not have a "regular" relationship? Nevertheless, a few years passed and still I secretly wanted to be with this man. Some people called it a soul-tie, which I didn't understand because we did not have sex, but nothing else made sense.

Then the day came that I had been waiting for, or so I thought. I found out that he had separated from that woman and came running straight to me. I was so excited, but he was moving extremely fast. I mean he wanted to have sex instantly. I told him we needed to wait and figure out our situation. I decided to go to an event with him and some friends. Long story short, he dropped me off last and we ended up in the back of the car and then went to his place. I knew what we had just done in the car, so when I went to his house, I knew what was coming, but still I said no.

Again, as I reflect, I can't help but acknowledge God's amazing grace. Even though I had strong feelings for him and I had allowed him to go places that no man had ever gone, I still said no. I believe God jumped in my body while on I was on his bed (totally naked) and made me extremely fearful, which was how I said no. I thank God for intervening that night because I found out the woman he separated from was pregnant and that could've been me.

It was hard to tell him no. I mean, this was the man of my dreams and finally he wanted to be with me; he was just on the rebound. At the time, I didn't know why I was compelled to keep saying "no", but God knew. He is such an Amazing, Amazing, Sovereign God! It says in Proverbs 3:5 and 6, "Trust in the LORD with all thine heart; and lean not unto thine own understanding. In all thy ways acknowledge him, and he shall direct thy paths". At this point and time in my life, I knew nothing about the bible – let along this scripture, but it was able to keep me protected.

Ten years passed and I was extremely bitter and brokenhearted. I had just started a new job where the alternative lifestyle was highly encouraged. I met this woman, which I ended up growing a crush. My family was telling me no, but my circumstances were saying yes. I kept it to myself for about a year; during this time, I was watching porn nonstop. What encouraged me to approach her is when "the man of my dreams" text me to say the time we'd spent together meant nothing to him. It was so hard to hear, so to feel better I put all my feelings into this woman instead of consulting God.

About three months later, I approached her. This woman was very attractive, but she was a stud (dominant lesbian). This amazed me as I wondered, if you chose this lifestyle to avoid being penetrated, why are you only attracted to studs? Anyway, once I approached her, I found out that she was involved, which made me upset. Though, I still found myself having strong sexual feelings for her I was able to say no when she asked me to be involved in a threesome.

God showed me so clearly with this situation that the "grass is not always greener on the other side". Case in point, I found out that this woman was only seeking me for sexual gratification because she too was on the rebound. Then I found out she got back with her girlfriend, which is when she asked me for the threesome. It's like she was finding sneaky ways to try to get me in the bedroom. Unbeknownst to me, she was a stalker (and a little crazy). She'd transferred her feelings from her girlfriend onto me just like I'd done. However, we both had to deal with the fact that neither one of us was willing to give the other person what she wanted. This caused a big problem between us and ultimately became a life-threatening situation.

We were both obsessed with one another, but I found non-hurtful ways to deal with it. She, on the other hand, was not having it. She tried to fight me and got everybody at my job to harass me. She told several lies about me harassing her and tried to get me fired several times. It became very uncomfortable to work because co-workers were calling me out of my name and I had no proof she caused the drama; no one that was willing to be on my side.

To add insult to injury, another lady who I thought was a cool, very attractive stud sided with her. I thought she wanted to be with me, but she just wanted sex from me to get revenge from a previous encounter. She recorded a private conversation we had and shared it with everybody at my job. It was so humiliating; everybody was laughing at me. I would have gotten the police involved, but I had no proof about the recording. To make matters even worse, both women teamed up and tried to beat me up and order me to be kidnapped. I thank God it did not happen. In my heart of hearts, I believe had they been successful it would have resulted in rape and my death.

This is when I started to acknowledge God in my situation. My God sent an angel to work for the company who began to pray with me about the situation. Within a month, the first woman either left or got fired, which I was so thankful for because now I only had to deal with second lady.

As time went on, me and my prayer partner began to pray and read scriptures and I started attending church...and enduring challenges. Somehow, the second lady got my phone number and started harassing me by phone. Once again, I had no proof because she was using Google calls, which are

Discipline

untraceable. But my God was still intervening because even though she was stalking me and had recorded me, the situation worked out for my good – just as it says in Romans 8:28.

Despite how bad this situation was, it could have been worse because she was trying to send the recording through social media, but to no avail. I surrendered to God and told Him I needed His help. He instructed me to quit the job, which left me unemployed and depressed. He told me so clearly, "If you don't leave. you will be destroyed". I gave them my two-week notice and on my last day somebody tried to run me over.

During this time, I found myself dealing with PTSD as well as being unemployed. However, God is still good because He had me become acquainted with a woman's group through my sister's church. I did not know this at the time, but God was prepping me to become a member of this church. Within a year, I no longer suffered with PTSD and I had joined the new church. Upon joining, I became acquainted with Pastor, First Lady and a wonderful congregation.

I noticed a complete change in myself where I became consumed with only praising God. I started paying my tithes and praying at 4 o'clock in the morning. I also made it my business to attend every service whether it was Bible Class, Sunday School, or Friday service. But when you decide to go to a new level in God, you must be ready for the new challenges and hardships that come with it. Admittedly, I was not ready. Yes, I was rooted in God, but not the Word. Both Matthew 4:4 and Luke 4:4 state, "man shall not live by bread alone, but by every word of God." I found out the hard way, you must know the word because when the enemy comes up against you, it is your most vital weapon.

While attending church, I learned that I could ask God for things and they would be given according to His will. So, I began to ask God for a husband, car, house, etc., not knowing that the devil heard those same prayers. It is very important to make sure that what you ask for is being presented from God and not the enemy.

Case in point, one of the things I asked God for was a husband. So when not one, but two different men appealed to me I thanked Him but was unsure which one was to be husband. Both men were very attractive and tall. One was black and the other was white. As time went on, I noticed both giving me this "I'm interested" look; however, neither presented themselves to ask me out on a date. Here is where I made my first error.

I assumed that the one who attended church would definitely be more husband material and so therefore I let my guard down and starting liking him. He was not coming up to me whatsoever, mind you, but I wasn't clear if he wanted me. He would just stare and make a lot of comments to me that led me to believe he only wanted me sexually. Not wanting to experience this again, I decided to hold out to see if he would approach me. During this same time, I was still looking at the other guy who was doing the same thing – staring at me like I was a piece of meat, yet not presenting himself to ask me out.

Here is my second error, actually, this should be number #1: I did not ask God to reveal the truth about either of these men from the beginning. I leaned to my own understanding and ended up growing feelings for the both without collecting the data. From the beginning, the red flags were there, but I chose to ignore them and go with what my flesh wanted and needed at that time. But God intervened and I'm glad He did because it turned out that both men were in desperate situations.

One was about to get married and only wanted me so he could have his first black woman experience before he got married. The other only wanted me so I could be his "primary source", a term I learned from Pastor RC Blakes. A primary source is usually who a narcissist sees as a caretaker. In other words, this guy, I believe was only looking at me for the purposes of taking care of him – not as a lover, more so as a parent.

Double the men, double the pain and now I'm praying for Double the blessing. Again I say, I should have asked God to reveal these men's true agendas at the onset. By asking God from the beginning, you are acknowledging His presence in your life and since He only wants the best for you, He will only tell you the truth. And when God tells you the truth, whether or not you want to hear it, you should obey.

So, even though I had not one but two men coming after me who were very attractive, I was still able to maintain self-control. It wasn't easy, but I did it. In the bible it says, there is nothing new under the sun. Many others have faced exactly the same problems before you. And although temptation seems irresistible, you can trust God to keep the temptation from becoming so strong that you can't stand up against it. He will show you how to escape temptation's power so that you can bear it.

Despite the temptations that came up against me from both men and women, God never put more on me that I could bear. This is why with every situation, God only allowed what I could handle at that moment, for which I am so grateful. Using discipline is one of the hardest things that God has asked of me, but in doing it, I know that I am going to be highly rewarded. That said, it is extremely difficult to look a person dead in the face and know that the devil sent them in your life to destroy you. However, I know that God will continue to give me the strength to get through it.

I believe God wants me to stay in the environment where I got hurt by both men for a season. He wants me to be able to keep a smile and a strong demeanor as if nothing has happened. I am finding that even though I did it before with the two women these situations are even harder because I didn't have the proof that would bring me closure. I don't have proof that the one man was trying to use me for sex and money. I don't have proof that the other only wanted sex to explore his curiosity with black women. The thing that hurts the most is that nobody believes me; both stories have been told to other people and nobody believes me. I decided that I will take a seat back from everything and allow God to search me, which describes my current situation.

Through this searching, God has informed me that I was dealing with some insecurities and that I was emotionally immature. This is why I have been attracting "grown boys" because I am a "grown girl". I had never heard of such a thing, but as I took a deeper look at how I responded to certain situations and how I handled my emotions, I could not help but to agree and not deny what God stated. I am now working on reinventing myself by working on my relationship with God and learning to love myself unconditionally.

Faith Walk:
Faith

Complete trust or confidence in someone or something

Jill Scott has a song called, A Long Walk, in which she describes all the possible things she can do along the way. Well, as an entrepreneur, I have found that while yes, long walks may be fun, faith walks are downright necessary. For almost a decade I have been an entrepreneur and a brick and mortar business owner for close to five years. Throughout this time, there have been many occasions where, not only did I NOT have the money to pay a bill, participate in an event or partake in festivities, but I had no clue when or if the money was coming, much less from where. But that was where my faith kicked in.

What is faith, you ask? According to Webster's dictionary, it is "complete trust or confidence in someone or something". Biblically speaking, "Faith is the substance of things hoped for and the evidence of things not seen" Hebrew 11:1. My personal definition, the one that has carried me thus far is kind of wrapped in Proverbs 3:5, "Trust in the Lord with all thine heart and lean not to thy own understanding". I can truly say that ALL my entrepreneurial ventures were about obedience – and faith. I'll never forget how my authorpreneurial journey started...

Although all my life I've loved writing, I never desired to be a published author. However, one night, God woke me from my sleep and told me I was going to write a book. If you've ever heard the voice of God, you know there is no mistaking His voice. This was not a conversation – more like instructions. He told me the name of the book, even the meaning behind it. My first book was called, Pleasing Your Partner: A Spiritual Guide to H.A.P.P.I.N.E.S.S. When He told me to write the word happiness, the instructions were to write it vertically so that each letter represented a word:

Humility

Assurance

Peace

Prosperity

Integrity

Newness

Endurance

Submission

Strength

He'd even taken the time to explain that the reason Submission was the first "s" word was because a true sign of strength is the ability to submit.

There was nothing conventional about my book. From a literary perspective, it was outright wrong. The title was the same size as the subtitle; the font choice wasn't standard; many issues were highlighted by traditional reviewers. Keep in mind that prior to this, I'd never written a book, so I wasn't familiar with the literary world – I just barely liked reading! So, everything, every element of this book was derived out of pure obedience.

I remember a representative from the publishing company I used calling me to say that I should add more content because it was only 42 pages. Please note, the trim size has since been changed to a 6x9, which by default, created additional pages, but the content remains the same. My response to her was simple, "I wrote what God told me to write and then I closed the book. To add anything else would be like telling Him that He needed my help, or what He said wasn't sufficient." She sounded completely baffled, and followed up with, "Are you sure?" I told her that that was the only thing of which I was sure!

Once the book was published, there were many naysayers who criticized the trim size choice and front cover; book reviewers said I should've shared personal testimonies because it read more like instructions. They said readers want to be able to identify with the author. My response to them was quite similar to what I'd told the publishing representative, "It's not for me to add". I knew God's voice, and although at the time I didn't know why I was instructed to write it, I believed that it had to be a purpose; otherwise, God wouldn't have used His time to instruct me to do it.

That same year, the book was celebrated in Ohio at the Dayton Book Expo; it was featured at the Baltimore Book Festival; it even became Award-Winning. I ranked #3 as the 2011 National Black Book Festival's Best New Author. I vividly remember telling my husband when traveling to Houston for the event, "I'm not sure what's going to come of this, but I know this isn't the end. God is using this to serve as a catalyst. Although I was extremely clueless of what my future would hold, the only thing I did know was that I would continue to trust God.

The following year, I published my first children's book, Four Girls: A Lot of Choices. The Chicago's Children Museum at Navy Pier featured me in their African American Heritage Exhibit. CBS Chicago recognized me as being one of "5 Indie Chicago Authors and Publishers to Watch Out For". By the end of the year, I'd release three more books (It's A Way to Say It All: How to Communicate with Your Partner; It's A Way to Say It All: How to Communicate with Your Kids; and Inspiration from A.B.O.V.E.), making it four books published in one year. The fifth title, Inspiration from A.B.O.V.E., became an International Award-Winner in 2013. Later that year, I created an organization purposed to help independent authors, Authors Promoting Success; this was definitively a faith move.

I knew nothing about having an organization. I couldn't imagine that it would be productive. It was a Moses moment as I wondered, "Who was I that anyone would want to listen to me?" However, I moved forward and in so doing, I have been able to collaborate with and mentor numerous authors across the country.

In 2014, I started my publishing company. Again, this was nothing I'd consciously thought about doing; it was more like a natural progression of things. People were asking me to share my experience as an author – how I'd done it; the process of publishing; etc. It was after helping one author that I had the epiphany of creating my own company. I'd done the research on the type of experience needed from a professional standpoint. Academically speaking, the preference was that one possessed a degree in Communication and have some business knowledge. Wouldn't you know that my bachelor's degree was in Communication and I had a master's degree in business administration? None of this was planned, but that's really my point. All of these decisions aligned with what God had in store for me because I wasn't able to foresee any of this. Knowing me, if I had known, I probably would've found a way to mess it up!

Later that year, God instructed me to open a bookstore. Now, although I'd been obedient up to this point, I couldn't help but to question Him, "Open a what?" I'd never owned a business before, so I had no idea the first thing about operating one. But again, His instructions were clear as day, "Go, and I'll show you what to do". As human, we prefer to know what to do before we go. I don't know that we perceive it as disobedience, more like not wanting to put ourselves in bad predicaments. But God was very specific, and I'd dealt with Him long enough to know His voice. So, if He said, "Go", even though I had no money and plenty of concerns, I went.

As I proceeded going to different neighborhoods looking for a venue, I'd hear a soft, "No, that's not it. Keep looking." One day, I was randomly cleaning out my wallet and found this piece of paper that was folded a million times over. I opened the paper to find a phone number written on it; it was to the leasing office inside of Ford City Mall. As soon as I saw the number, I remember having written it four years earlier when I worked for Radio Shack (the year was 2011 and I'd just published my first book).

At that time, there was a kiosk outside of the store and a man who sold CDs. I remember thinking that one day I would get my own kiosk to sell my books. As I was going home that day, the number was posted in the foyer and I wrote it down and tucked it in my wallet. I'd though no more about it – until this day. I picked up the phone to call the number; to my surprise, it still worked.

I spoke with the leasing manager and shared my

idea (God's instruction) with her. She informed me that it had been over a decade since the last time they'd housed a bookstore. She asked my budget; when I told her, she responded that it might be enough to get a small space, maybe 800 square feet, which was okay with me. I initially saw the space in the fall of 2014. She wanted me to purchase it then, but God had told me not until April 2015. So, that's what I told her. She told me that she wouldn't be able to promise the space would still be available then to which I replied, "If it's meant for me, it will still be here." I called her in December, and the space was gone. However, I continued to believe and told God, "Now, I know you told me to go there, and I know you said April, and I also know you heard her say that the space is no longer available. So, if you want me to open the store in that mall, you have to work it out".

In February, the lady called to inform me they had another space to open that was twice the size as the original space. If I liked it, they could give it to me for the same price; obviously, I jumped at the chance. I went to look at the space and was very impressed. The young lady told me that they were undergoing a management change, so she'd have to pitch my concept to the new owner and get back to me. She called back to say that the owner didn't want to give me either space; I asked what happened. She said, "Well, actually, she loved your idea so much that she wanted to give you an entirely different space!" I kept listening, now in total disbelief. She continued, "Didn't you say you once worked for Radio Shack?" I replied with a simple, "Yes". She said, "Well, I guess it's a total 180 for you because that's the space she wants to give you".

Before I allowed myself to get too excited, I asked her the price. She said, "That's the thing. She's going to give it to you for the same price." Just in case you didn't catch that, let me make it plain. I ultimately got a location that was three times as big as the original space for the EXACT SAME PRICE! Had I doubted any of God's instructions, I would not have had the same outcome. Had I done what the lady was prompting me to do, I would have gotten a store that was 800 square feet off to the side of the mall. However, by trusting God and implementing my faith, I received a store that was over 2500 square feet on the main strip of the mall!

I could go on, because believe me, there's more, but I think you get the point. Although this was a glimpse of my entrepreneurial journey, no matter what capacity of life you present, if you have faith and are not afraid to exercise it, the end will always be the same. You will come out victorious. All God wants is for us to have faith, listen and obey His voice. I'm a witness that if you can manage to do that, He will take care of the rest!

Mary Hale

Retired Revenue Agent. Evangelist, Prophetess, wife, mother, grandmother, entrepreneur and proud award-winning published author of the Speak to My Heart Book Series released in 2018.

Born in Memphis, TN, I have always enjoyed the arts. When I'm not taking care of my family, I find reading, writing, and listening to music to be very comforting. My favorite book is the Bible; my favorite Gospel artist is Marvin Sapp. Like his song states, I believes that without God, I "Never Would've Made It" this far in my life's journey and I am always looking forward for the next journey.

Other Books by Mary Hale:
Emotional Baggage ~ *The Formation of My Walls*
The Walls of My Heart ~ *The Castle of My Heart*

Oeinna Jackson

First time author. Mother of 3. Daughter. Sister. Mentor. Student.

Born and raised in Chicago, Oeinna loves to travel, enjoys spending time with her family and learning more about the world as well as herself. Although this is her first writing project, it won't be her last!

Valorie Tatum

Valorie Tatum is a native of Chicago. She received her bachelor's degree from National Louis University's School of Education, as well as a certification in pharmacology from Kennedy King College. Currently, Valorie teaches special education.

Other Books by Valorie Tatum:
Rita Rabbit & The Runaway Pie
Who Would You Tell: A Guide to Help Overcome Bullying
Beyond Being Valorie
Once Upon A Time... I Was Never Young
God Call God Order
Mission, Vision & Pedagogy

International Award-Winning Author
Toneal M. Jackson

Toneal M. Jackson is a National and International Award-Winning Author; Publisher; and Inspirational Speaker. She is the founder of Artists Promoting Success, an organization that educates indies on the business of being entrepreneurs as well as provides platforms for exposure. She's also the founder of #ImGladToBeAWoman, an organization that empowers women regardless of age, race, relationship or economic status.

In 2012, CBS Chicago named her one of "5 Indie Authors and Publishers to Watch Out For". Toneal was inducted into the Young Women's Professional League in 2016 and POWER (Professional Organization of Women of Excellence Recognized) in 2018. In 2019, she received the I Change Nations Award for her work in the literary industry. For more on Toneal, visit: www.AWEInspiringCoach.com

Other Books by Toneal M. Jackson:

Pleasing Your Partner: A Spiritual Guide to
H.A.P.P.I.N.E.S.S.
Four Girls: A Lot of Choices
Four Girls Learn Their Colors
It's A Way to Say It All: How to Communicate with
Your Kids
It's A Way to Say It All: How to Communicate with
Your Partner
Growing Up to be Happy
She's Out. I'm In
Inspiration from A.B.O.V.E.
Learning to Love Me
Love Me…Please
Being an Authorpreneur: How to Succeed
in the Book Business
The Race to the Ring: The Seven Cs of a
Successful Courtship
Praising through the Pandemic

About Toneal M. Jackson

www.ingramcontent.com/pod-product-compliance
Lightning Source LLC
LaVergne TN
LVHW051700080426
835511LV00017B/2644